ABOUT THE AUTHOR

Rushika Wick is a poet, doctor and Children's Rights advocate who is interested in how social structures and relationships impact the body. She has performed with the Cold Lips Magazine collective in London, Rough Night Press (Amsterdam) and Skylark (Norwich) communities. Her work has been published in literary magazines including *Ambit*, *Datableed* and *Tentacular* and within anthologies including *Fool-saint* (Tangerine Press), *Alter Egos* (Bad Betty Press) and *Smear* (Andrews McMeel). She is delighted to have Verve publishing her first collection *Afterlife As Trash*.

Website: https://rushikawick.com
Instagram: @rushikawick

'The poems in Rushika Wick's debut collection are like little time bombs, packed with shocking and beautiful truths about how we live, what and who we love, how we die. They often feel as if they've been translated from a mysterious language or passed on in whispers – their imagery is so rich and strange and compressed – but always in the moment and pushing against conventional lyric and form. She approaches her subjects with a forensic eye and a deft scalpel, getting to the heart of what's vital.' - *Tamar Yoseloff*

'Rushika Wick's sensational debut pops with blistering satire and psychedelic detail. In 'a time that calls for swords not ink', this book's code-switching, unreliable narrator shines a light on all that is absurd, tragic and fabulous about being human.'
- *Amy Acre*

'A mesmerising collection filled with heart and magnetic wonder.'
- *Greta Bellamacina*

'Her poems grow in the mind of the reader, examining the sustainability of humanity as it is ... each poem captures the moment before everything explodes.' - *Ana Seferovic*

Rushika Wick
Afterlife As Trash

VERVE
POETRY PRESS
BIRMINGHAM

PUBLISHED BY VERVE POETRY PRESS
https://vervepoetrypress.com
mail@vervepoetrypress.com

FIRST PUBLISHED APR 2021

Printed and bound in the UK
by ImprintDigital, Exeter

ISBN: 978-1-912565-56-6

Cover Art by Juli About - Juliabout.wix.com/ceramique

"I felt a kind of vertigo, as if I were merely plunging from one world to another, and in each I arrived shortly after the end of the world had taken place."
— Italo Calvino, *If on a Winter's Night a Traveler*

"The inferno of the living is not something that will be; if there is one, it is what is already here, the inferno where we live every day, that we form by being together. There are two ways to escape suffering it. The first is easy for many: accept the inferno and become such a part of it that you can no longer see it. The second is risky and demands constant vigilance and apprehension: seek and learn to recognize who and what, in the midst of inferno, are not inferno, then make them endure, give them space."
— Italo Calvino, *Invisible Cities*

CONTENTS

Acknowledgements

Afterlife
As Trash

Tumbling plastic bag
holding so much yesterday
for such a short time.

Diaries Of An Artist In Hiding

I am the president
I tell myself out loud in the car
on the way to work as a social experiment,
I am the president I am the president
by the end of the journey I am taller, fatter,
dreaming of an André Breton republic and Cuban cigars.

The broader view is my poetry of hagiography,
I am becoming beatific,
rise above most things -
a swallow filled with helium
soon to feel altitude sickness.
Really the experiment is myself,
there are no controls that I am aware of
it's a pretty state of affairs
can do what I want when I want and so on.

I am Matisse with a charcoal
drawing on the walls from my sick bed today.
The flu is viral and I am kept inside
a glass cloche of yellow and pink spring blooms.
More work is needed I tell myself,
only the lines, the forms, the space can reveal the truth absolute
straight from a Russian Vodka God or my dancing hands,
no deviation from the discipline of the line.
Charcoal dust falls to the concrete floor.

I am romantic on Tuesday
a love letter from Camille to Rodin
filled with the language of marble,
flowering fingers, fractures,
scatters of light picking out human form.
Rasps and rifflers fall from cramped hands
warming each other beneath dust sheets.

Most days I have concealed myself so well
that I am free to lie in a dark space,
expecting nothing but the occasional
levitation of a knife or
corkscrewing of a bird feeder.
I am becoming the weather.
I hear of snow on the radio,
next day it falls on cherry blossom,
petals and ice confuse.
Oh the joys of such freedom!

This morning I am a badger
I have an earthen dwelling and
have bitten you for coming too close
unheeding of the clear warnings.
Soon I will *piss en plein air* and
find some unwanted dog food and
be happy.

The experiment is boundless
like the imagination of a new subspecies
of giant squid,
immeasurable and brilliant,
its owner perceived as a delicacy.

ULTRAMARINE PINK PV15

1

Can you remember that shade of Angel Delight?
It was the time of Michael Knight & pixie boots.
But I could not focus, reeling from the pink balloon
reminding me of intensive care ventilators
& a Dutch sex doll I had seen at an installation
sitting with a vase of giant peonies,
each like a face, sympathetic to her escape
from a canal-side bedroom stained with tobacco.
I remembered the school trip to Amsterdam
where I learned that sex is not a thing of beauty in itself,
but could look like a multi-pack of Salt 'n' Shake,
each packet with its own blue sachet
containing exactly 0.6g of salt.

2

Sex is not a thing of beauty in itself. It is a plastic bag caught in the
wind, seeking headlights. It is half a breath, a self-portrait. A white
porcelain heart clamped between legs. It is a machine, a salt lick in
the field - solid as animals come by, or bitter greens for health. It is
a clock, a severed oyster, a dream of Orpheus or physical exercise.
It is smearing blue make-up across the face and not looking down.
It is sleep walking. Feigning sleep. Electrocution from a plug socket.
Turning a musty page. It is not Freud & the patriarchy. It is biting
filled candy until it leaks. Falling sequins. A sick bag. A footnote.
The beast whose face is faceless, a burning wound. A salve. Bird
entrails strung out across the lawn. It is both a whistle & a trained
dog, a cracked jug seeping water.

Deus Ex Machina

Impossible sunflowers grow in the hard corridor
between the road and tower block.
They are soft velvet toys,
hyper-real, abandoned by gardeners.
Summer is brash and almost over like youth.

Citrine light seeps through the office window.
Cigarette-ends and hole-punch confetti litter the exit.
She wonders how to make her money stretch
beyond rent and a bag of happy-face waffles,
tired legs soak up heat as she leans against a wall.

There is so much sunshine she would be rich if she could bottle it,
but even this is an unaffordable expense.

The walls of her room are covered
in monochrome volcanoes and flying cranes.
She writes on scraps of paper as night crumples the sky,
inside this machine which whirrs without end,
walls and ceiling move toward each other.
She has taught herself how to wake just in time,
gasping.

The Party

Some of these people travelled for miles to come and stand in the burning sun, in belief.

To stand together, united against the dragging through fields, the hangings, the spitting on children the taking of women like property.

What makes one movement a success and another not? Are we not facing the very worst future right now?

It was the kind of conversation where people living in comfortable homes full of art and fruit bowls confess that the time is such that they would be able to kill their political leader, should the opportunity arise, for the greater good. This then creates some solidarity at the party but also deep discomfort. And then someone else who has had less wine asks about steps of othering and the fading of moral lines.

Others said that finally they had been allowed the time (because of reaching a certain stability or point in their careers) to become fully practicing witches and what a joy this was. They had even been able to do a field trip to Mexico to source blank tongues and scrape gilt off Madonnas at night.

The Friends

I know you're tired, but believe me it's not what it looks like.
I know, because I'm older. When you're older, your consciousness has had
more time to spread out further, into more territories and to merge into
those of others - even sea-life and plants.
Please don't think I'm being condescending.

Well, you are.

Look, why not try having an attitude like that of Europeans when a
baby starts prattling in a restaurant? Rather than irritation, there is
a cultured delight at the anarchy, the art of pure communication. I am
communicating purely with you.

Go on.

I see your tiredness and I want you to work at using it, like a catalyst.
Your body is still connected to your mind - there are not many like you
left.
Are my eyelashes okay by the way?

Yeh they look good. You are so full of shit though! Why are you placing
me in some kind of special flock - you know I hate that. Both 'flocks' and
'specials'.
In fact, tell me why should I bother listening to you - you`re not even a
witch yet!

Because of compassion.

Because of compassion? What does that even mean?

We have been compassionate toward each other, always.

I suppose it's true - we have always treated each other kindly, including with probiotics and sudden gifts, which is rare these days.

And authenticity.

Okay. Our friendship is authentic. You are authentic. Hah, I do love the way you invent new names all the time and post brash selfies! Like the one where you wore pale green lipstick and looked like a tropical fish - remember? I felt that I really understood what you were trying to say there, that it was important, like it could not be articulated better any other way *holds hands in her own*, I mean it.

You see...

Yeah, so maybe I should listen to you. At least we get each other.

But wait while I unwrap this, I'm starved and can't eat this party food. Come, move a bit to the left so the hosts can`t see me - it`s kinda rude of me, no?
They're serving human bone meal canapés to reduce waste. And as a witch in training this sort of food is not permitted, too high in regrets.

So let's hear the wisdom then.

So, what I say is that your tiredness is like that of a hundred jewels in the night. They do not need to move to catch the light. They can still dazzle. Because of their nature - they have endured the highest tectonic pressures and heats. It has formed them and they too are exhausted. And they feel sick to fracture from all the blood lost by humans because of their simple ability to trap light.
So take your tiredness, stuff it into an old glass jar and throw it into the street, into the crowd. Go home to watch the bedazzling through your window. You will feel relief and can continue with your own work.
This is a spell - a kinda basic one. Good though.

My own work. Yeah. I see what you're saying. Never enough time for that.
Okay I'll try it as it`s one of your first and you are my best girl.
This is so live!
Sit down, Elvis.

The Dog

God is my best friend - that is what happens in palindromes if there are two sentient subjects. It's quite touching. They are really not benevolent which is a massive relief bc otherwise we are all fucked. They are sometimes emotionally unavailable which can be hard but you have to understand Their childhood was exceptional. Full of weird toys that came to life and a pet snake which was sick everywhere and cost Them a fortune in veterinary bills. No parents, just a void of space-time.

God is always saying that I'm a giver not a taker and I need to get the balance right otherwise people will walk all over me and even try to sext me when I prefer the more direct ways in the forest surrounded by wood anemones.

One thing I hate about Them is their overbearing perfume - sodden with notes of freesia and rose. It's derivative and completely unnecessary as They have all the best scents like rain on dry earth and hot liver. I've said it to Their face. They won't listen. Anyway I'm talking about Them to deflect the attention away from me and bc usually that's what the journos are after. You are one of them, aren't you? Can you scratch my back for me? I can`t reach between my shoulder blades.

The Flea

I can't keep still ***waves four limbs around magnanimously***
I have that condition bc my mother drank too much it's a little bit
tragic *n`est ce pas?* ***stands on head*** But if not for her I wouldn't
be in the circus and this is my *raison d'être,****single cartwheel***
the spirit of circus is my muse! ***back on rear two legs waving
other limbs in windmill*** I can't blame her bc all one wants
as a kid is two parents who don't treat each other or you like shit
dusts hands off even better, ones whose eyes sparkle sometimes - *magnifique-* ***head spin*** - not in the movies but at the end
of a long rainy day when it`s cold *comme ça* and they can still spar-
kle their eyes after all that ***strokes chin***. All the labouring away
for a spot to call home and a Friday night out, so what if that's
lubricated by the gin? ***double head spin*** *Oh là là!*
If that's what it takes to endure the boring home-keeping, a
nursing job, the rollercoaster ride of my father`s passions *mais oui*
they had that sparkly eye I told you of ...***moon walks*** I believe
neurodiversité is enabling the best art, *enfin* we break away from that
dull canon and into the circus canon! Plenty of gunpowder and
pzazz and all that jazz but it must be relevant and *peut-être futuriste*
so here we are without the waxed moustaches and berets and a
new language ***curls into a ball*** if you can`t control your
emotions you may as well control your double back-flip where at
least you have some chance of landing *bien sûr* I have to go now
merci!

Love Island

I don't know if we are as nature intended.
You say we left the garden a while back.
Vodka & bath water
at the edge of the bandwidth. *Hold it together, girl.*

The sky is a conversation.
A storm blows our conjunction indigo
& the cold is ever,
a pricking geography.

I have to go home to get clothes
I tell him. *Join up the dots of Orion.*
On the street, preachers abound.
Peaches. Vipers. Vast jokes about dolls.

People can afford God & a drink.
Besides belief is a type of happiness
as a crystal splits light
& eyes are drawn to giant circle earrings.

Blind people stagger past. *Look at the birds,*
I tell myself, *they are an anchor.*
I am froth, sitting on the surface
breathing smog, from an autumn cylinder.

Strangers laugh, reassured by the pace of the day.
Can't they see what is happening?
You ask me questions that expose
our bones, vibrating with calcium.

Your teeth, cyanide white & eventual,
a tender cover on my neck.
Let's lie in the planetarium,
count electric muses you say.

I hold you in disbelief, loved-up to the hilt.

It Is Raining And Everyone Is Fading

I reach the middle of the road.
Out of the corner of my eye, a motorbike
in the wrong lane, arriving at speed,
a picture book of flesh and displayed skull,
leather jacket embroidered with marigolds,
Día de los Muertos.

I dismiss this.
There are rules in this country after all.

I descend the steps in rain
huddle between kiosk and shelter, a no-man's land
of flower-box art and coffee ads.
Commuters fringe the platform
watching arrival times.

I wonder about the use of the first person
and if there are too many poets for a time
that calls for swords not ink.

I am wondering if my wondering is a diagnosis in itself.

Pissoirs are back in fashion and
immigrants are turned away.

How the bitterness of tea can be softened by sugar.

On the train there is advice on the loudspeaker,
donate online to a homeless charity -
a diversion from looking humans in the eyes.

On the escalator
I want to shout

I am a robot!
but my safety programming is prohibitive.
I wish to see teeth line the automatic doors
to make it all a bit alive,

watch metal bite.

*Curb confetti of
steamed rice and scattered bird bones.
So many hungry.*

Cut-ups

(A sex worker & a seamstress across two times, Norwich)

Night has its own rules,
unseen vistas packed
into a velvet walnut,

sounds of emptying rubbish &
thrift-shop stilettos are traceable,
edged like fireworks & Novocaine.

She sits at the table in candlelight, bone needle between fingers.

Night's landscape is disowned,
a pleated skirt of new space,
a canvas for rituals.

She is here & not here.

Playing a game in the ruins of light,
waking with gull cries & strangers
pulling through her hair &
she is asexual, feels a new weight.
This is a safe place, safer than yesterday.

A dart of blue thread along the hem...

What would Kathy Acker do with a dead body?
She'd put it to work, tongue in cheek,
get a tattoo & charge sad men.

Pricks her finger, stinging is better than a flowering bruise.

It would cover the sparking coffee,
the library fines, the rent,

only soft bodies waiting to be hurt
into existence,
dissolving in rims of salt,
turning to marble at dawn.

Runs a stitch back along the whalebone, the girl must be of womanly form.

Some of her friends will not survive this season.
Their children, loved from afar & ignorant.

She once wore her mistress' evening gown
& the weight of it
dragged on her rosary ribs, made her gasp for air
made her surely retch.

Elite Members Of The Momentariat

Behold the fallen woman!
Hyper-lashes in smears & marbled thighs -
a museum. Yet some small voice speaks out
restore all processes of change, sky-born & elemental -
there is nothing to love about unlined faces
 unless within motherly hope.

Look in one mirror for decay
yet two for infinity, an elegant mathematics.
Swallow it, the world is bigger than a face
the thousand ships were ready to launch
though it must be said the curve of her eyebrows
obeyed the golden section.

Notice that exquisite Japanese face cream
is nothing more than poetry & dust.
You could blush more from a song
or from eating print, all demi-plumes
plucked from a Wildean dream,
sordid & complete, an ellipse of light.

In a magazine -
how fasting fires the metabolism
turns apples to pears,

forgetting how mouthfuls of nothing
bring one closer to heaven
in parabolas & diamonds of projected daylight.
Step by step, bones grow weightless
like wings spun from a 3D printer
& mind is a harmony,

but let's face it, who would believe that
outside of a death sentence?
Can we ever learn how to experience poetry
without the presence of ghosts?*

---

*Attribution to The Color of Pomegranates script by Sergei Parajanov
(1969) celebrating the Armenian poet Սայաթ-Նովա (Armenian)
سایات‌نووا (Azeri/Perisan) საიათნოვა (Georgian) known in English as
Sayat Nova (1712-1795).

THE THOUGHTS OF VALERIE SOLANAS (in the minute before shooting Warhol and the minute after)

Freak! Read the S.C.U.M. manifesto!
You reek of distilled Paris
and privilege
and those neat risograph prints
ricochet with linear patriarchy,
the oppression of pressed paper
produced in moneyed parody.

Your hand is a distant memory in your work,
let it make true marks like a philosopher again!
I swear I have lived honestly;
let my words be a gift to you.

You and your wife – 'the tape recorder'
for you (of all people) get what 'wife' is;
a silent witness, a recipient, a perpetrator,
same as whores,
same as all of us
with intact chromosomes
being fucked roughly
like islands in storms.

Yellow is the colour of the future,
a hooker's shirt and guess what
I'm wearing it today
but have no sex at all and yes
I weep for you
and your weary womb-envy.

I think about what makes you a success,
and me, a sideshow, an extra.

Tricks and mantras for a living
skin and bone on skin and bone
and the rickety-tick of a typewriter
drawing a thread of sound
through an unlit room
like an electric shock in Bellevue
reserved for the dissenting undead.

SUNLIT GUNSHOT

Let's call this a hysterectomy
of sorts, the language of violence
has its own vowel sounds
and is smokeless like cordite,
as bright as junk-light,

you were sharkish
when last in the diner
and it made me uneasy –
you thought my anger was
a bloodhound sniffing out
plagiarism, appropriation,

when really what broke me
was the carelessness
of misplacement
which -nota bene –
only the patriarchy can afford.

I leave you a paper bag
with my address book –
ring my friends,
call in my debtors,
clamp the sanitary pad
to your bleeding spleen
Peroxide Jesus, and I'll see you
on the other side.

Why I Cannot Watch Most Films Twice

It's awkward when you ask if I want to see *Ghostbusters* again
because I said no already three times so it's humiliating for us both.

As I am both living and dying every day I wish only for
the extraordinary.

Also, please realise that no matter how funny, I object to the
vacuum suction of spirits in all their fragile forms. *Stay Puft*
reminds me of people in American Diners who don't see their real
reflections in the windows. Everyone's frightened of *Stay Puft*
because of his *size* - just thinking about this gives me a twitchy eye.

It's not a matter of self-control you know, it's more like life is out
of control, has been a bitch in some way. Don't make me spell this
out, you're smart enough.

I like films that I haven't seen before, quiet ones about women and
the lives of animals. That's the truth.

Old yellow sweatshirt
a singing canary, slumps
mute on the pavement

Section 2 Of The Mental Health Act

this violent quill outlines the outliers
this spectral trill warbles twice off my bitten tongue
until the section of dodecahedron faces us again
with all its flying pills and ice-teeth and
shuddering I know these strings thinning into
nylon strands snap-snapping in sun
swooned-truth in childhood but
all-ears are soon brutalised
and barricades mounted quicker than Italian crema
in a sex demonstration have you got the right papers
they write in shorthand some things about love
from temples in a democracy in a democracy
everyone would be a friend and
the dark sow would not roll in the fallow
sewing itself with blue silk surgically
a gift to the people from Orwell and portents
would be meaningful penetrating
dead spines entwined with milk-whistles and
forget-me-nots honestly it's safer in a bar waiting
on a drink wanting all to burn to clear it out
one blue whale excretion of ambergris
one bingo-hall sigh like a flamingo throat retch
or squirting plant food in plastic packets into
vase-water delaying floral death waste
water softer than the thin nighties of my daytime
hovering luckless and moving through
the shifting walls of Unit 5 night shift
round vending machines in pale tea waterfalls
washing it all out washing hung out to dry on the taut line
femoral line access to all places but there's
no geography left access is a false consent

like confetti philosophy
or the word NICE printed how on the biscuit
why on the biscuit
like an ingestion design on autonomy
28 days in

Notes on the poem
The poem is in the voice of a great mind who suffers from REDACTION. During times of REDACTION she creates a new language of trauma and philosophy, symbols brought into existence to be read.

Hair

"I had only one desire: to dismember it. To see of what it was made...."
- Toni Morrison

You brushed her hair when your mother was ill,
sunlit silk, hot sand slipping through fingers by the creek,
not of burnt sugar spun in air.
You stared at it, trying to make some of the gold go into you,
she asked you what you were doing.
Body cane-straight so that when she wore dresses,
they hung like elegant washing, left to dry.
Calico and soap, Sunday milk,
the cat with golden eyes watching the
relentless washing and scrubbing until skin split
to white flesh.

Parakeet Earrings

On the night train to Berlin
a traveller drops a book,
The Waste Land.
Earrings of chartreuse birds,
home a thousand miles away,
mountains trailed by
flak and chemical rain.

She reaches to the floor.
Worn as talismans or a forest tonic
a taking-in, like the green enema
she queues for on Mondays,
drowning in the Amazon
washing away her past
and those little wrong cells.

Each bird is slightly different.
The beak on the left is red flecked with gold,
the curve of the breast is sharper.
The right piece is heavy,
pulls on her lobe.

Though it is late, her twin sister calls
offering perfume and the gift of marrow,
avoiding the names of their dead,
earth hung with sulphur.

Empty box of cigs,
each smoke a thread to the stars.
Ash dancing with light.

The Pill

Upper*; stimulant
eg cocaine, amphetamines/
situated on higher ground/
above another part/ higher
in place/ position/ pitch/ scale,
the parts of a boot or shoe above the sole/
superior in rank / dignity/ station
at another level/ more northerly/ further from the sea,
can you see the Aurora Borealis - green ribbons pulsing/
disturbances in the magnetosphere caused by solar wind,
do we deserve to see nature regardless of rank/ station/ dignity
we are made of plasma and drugs just like those
from the other kingdoms, no different, life is always prefaced
and terminal, we are hired to perform all the
dances on the road, can you feel that bass drop
those born with more synaptic glue feel more deeply, are they
higher/ superior all the time/ privileged/ further from the sea
Downer*; drug that makes you feel calmer / closer to the sea
a depressant or tranquilising drug, eg barbiturates/ a dispiriting or
depressing experience or factor eg fascism/ racism
inviting use of an upper/ a period of consistent failure
inviting use of an upper/ a cow or other animal that has fallen
and cannot get to its feet unaided/ homelessness/
broken wheelchair/ fatal stab wound to chest
inviting use of a downer and then an upper,
look at the dim LEDs in the neon awning,
misfortune/ drag/ bad trip/ raw deal,
once read in tea-leaves by the season`s
drag queen in Bournemouth; it was raining
heavily and hearts were sodden
and reaching toward the sea,
too many can stop you
breathing

*Side effects

Uppers:

- Rapid heart rate, sense of location of the heart, heart becomes a musical instrument, expansion of the heart, failure to love, heart failure

- Dizziness, sense of physical spinning overrides societal spinning & individual feels a heightened sense of control, fun, fallibility enabling fun, free entry

- Insomnia, wakefulness during sleep counteracting sleep fulness when awake, go to settings, zero hours to waste, go to settings, lucid dreaming, physical advantage in the timescape

Downers:

- Fatigue, enforced resting, taking control of stress that is structural in cause, soft pillows, nests, reason not to perform gender-stereotyped roles

- Impairment of memory, improvement of remaining memory, quality not quantity, wait in economical state until next software update not seeking connection speed increase, memories of ebbing anxiety

- Shallow breathing, reduced NO2 intake, reduced particulate intake, adaptive in hotter weather, retention of higher percent of the self

After Reading A Rewilding Book

She feels a greening. Pods of black dots quake like tadpoles in a
storm, the wind moving spent poppy heads in the garden.
Branches weave together, twisted veins of phloem.

She walks inside to the kitchen, unsettled by the room which is
small and incomprehensible. Mycelium softness bowls out across
the vast plate in her hand. Looking closer, the fine threads sway in
the breeze of breath. In a bowl sits a petrified pomegranate,
journeying to marble. The pink-red is bleaching out, leaving an
almost buff streak of Gothic hairdo. There is a faint scent of
sourness.

A spider plant nursery hangs from elegant pots, trembling. The
window gives onto fern fronds flush against glass, unravelling.
A booming of power from wet and light. Not even the tips are
brown. Petals crash in vermillion down to the sand, sand-smell
of hot rock and thoughts of bodies. She presses her face to the
window which is stuck, has not been opened for years in this quiet
corner of France. One further along is open and a little pale spider
descends along the wooden frame. The glass is cool like seawater.

There is a knock at the door, she peels her tendrils off the surface
and tries to walk over but the soles of her feet cannot move, dusty
rootlets probe their way down cracking through the terracotta tiles.
She is feeling... Better. She extends into coffee earth, past worms
making shapes of letters, threads herself between grass rhizomes.
Her mind feels well, starts to open up until it catches all the light
and brims colour into the room.

Sam she calls out, knowing her friend has no key, knowing she will
not reach him.

Sam`s ear is pushed to the door wondering what's taking so long. He hears a creaking like branches in wind, which become louder over time as a branch connects itself to the door and the door is slowly eased off its hinges.

He steps inside and sees her face in new leaves, hears her sighing in relief.

Baba Yaga In Her Life As A Teacher

Eyes are cellophaned from sleep.
She is sipping green milk in a Kimono,
turning the pages of a new book.

Men from the nettles
blister about the colour of her morning, her nails,
with invectives caustic as new moons
rising on hot skin. They see
veins like tiny skulls on her eyelids.

Morning sun moves
across the table in sequence,
picking out a mortar,
her crocus-skinned hand,
fallen sequins from a midnight shift.

They watch her
through the net curtain veil
whilst she observes light and shadow
trawl across the kitchen floor,
an underwater disco
hosting memories like sad fish
from when the music was hard and
people cried softly in the toilets, in love.

First lesson on Monday -
teenage boys are picked apart
unpeeled layer by layer,
pale gleaming onions in magic light
lying in dust.
A great eye is chalked upon the board
the eye of a magnificent horse and everyone is quiet now.
Even the men turn back for home
where they will wipe their noses on dirt sleeves, unobserved.

The Time An Eagle

I will not retell a myth –
how a broken egg
builds the strings of our arteries
quivering with pump sunset.
I will not tell you of the event horizon
of a cuckoo's morning call,
oiled and perfect,
spreading like a sheen on a pool
nor of future tangled in the witch-hedgerow
below sparks of plum, naked in the sun.
Such talking has been swallowed
and thrown up again and again
by men.
Instead, the sky riots,
new writings appear in cracks of earth
to hard-press the ear against.
An aging sun flits across the eye of a crow,
furious as the day.
The animals are laughing.
Narcissus faints in amongst the ferns,
they piss on him below the vertigo of dusk.
Smell the rising sulphur, watch life - how it
starts and starts
without fear.
The night is quiet.
A powdered bonbon of blue.
The time, an eagle.

Love Can Be Found In The Ruins

in the care it took to carve the marble -
her fingers bled
& like chiselling air but it was done,
in graffiti of runes & capitals
exploding in quiet alleys.
Love resides in broken cups, fragments like milk teeth,
once cradled by her lover's hands
& bringing warmth to her morning mouth.
Love is in the window
where she used to look out on gardens
filled with oranges and weeds,
on the splintered wooden floor
she'd whirled upon countless times,
in the cracked plaster, the dust
holds a million tiny conversations
like particles of gold.
Where she opens a desk and finds
her name engraved in the heart of it.

My Identical Twin

is weeping for clean air
iced- teeth calving on
clamped champagne glass
& biting down on too-brittle candy
lest it's the last good thing ever.

It's just sugar
but she'll take it alright.
Like the line she took/
the line she read
before the swerve on the road
shattering chronology
a nothing-to-lose preface
committing her.

She tried books as gum shields
but still the enamel splintered.
If only she'd had a nervous breakdown,
something with room for recovery,
it is said we need more nervous breakdowns.
& if her lips crushed the windscreen
they chose it
not the other way round.

or laughter for some years prior to death,
like a slack trampoline worn out in childhood
now collecting leaves.

On opening the thoracic cavity
and cutting through the pleura
the lung tissues were macroscopically normal.

However, under the microscope the alveolar walls
were found to be shot full of planetary elements of mercury,
tiny droplets suspended in a
wash of pity and water which shared
the composition of the Atlantic from
a sunlit swim last summer.

The diaphragm was found to be flaccid
and likely had been ineffectual in facilitating deep respiration

or laughter for some years prior to death,
like a slack trampoline worn out in childhood
now collecting leaves.

Detailed examination of the great arteries was unremarkable,
however, dissection of the heart
surprisingly revealed that it was devoid of arterial blood
(the really red stuff of balloons and hibiscus)
it was so empty that you could hear
footsteps echoing from one chamber
to the next. It was like a closed museum
and on closer examination
was short-circuiting and making
an old telephone ring.

On entry into the abdominal cavity,
the spleen was the size of a beluga's
and filled with plastic stars and critiques.
Nothing could get through it, nothing.

(The coroner became melancholic
just contemplating it.
He had started a series of drawings about it all.)

My twin always told me to
swallow pride & collect
scraps of freedom on the floor.

Aren't you tired of pretending? She said.

I listened to her occasionally
because of rivalry & noise,
but now that's all I think of
in the important moments
of these quickening days.

!!!!//////////~
Vocal Tics
!!!!!!!! ~~~****~~~~~~2222

The woman's
voice
started to drone
and she   ""

giggled in between   delivering dry facts,
as if in embarrassment at   the ridiculousness of her
plight, but then the giggles   became more pronounced

and hysterical like she was trying to
communicate
something
much harder, a secret,   an edge on
which her whole precarious life was   balanced,
and then new sounds   **interspersed her**
speech   **jumping in** whenever
there was a   gap, **humming**
in self-deprecation   and
whooping in   exhilaration,
as if some   more essential part
of her   needed out,
needed an   ether to ride, and
our tired   minds were tripping
through   this forest wondering
if the sounds   were ours or hers
and wondering   how to see more sky whilst
not cutting down trees   and then
her chest opened up   and tiny birds flew out
and around the room   and we wished
that we too had   birds inside of us.

51

And then birds flew out of her ch e *V* s   t

In The Tower That Night

Part 1 - Plans For Survival

And what happened after the eviction from their bodies?
A mother and son embrace,
twenty floors up, the heat bowing girders,
the lament of the building.
A breath ago, she filled the bath with water,
noticed the shampoo had run out.

The scent of lavender is dense.
Hair strands intertwine, glow like tungsten wire.
She enfolds her son, his face
ruby light.

The eye is drawn
now to wreckage, ears to the sound of
hymns shot through with particles of gold
reticular and wanting,
grasping hands lifting skyward.

Part 2 - The Building Has The Ghost Of A Blue Whale

Owners of the estate - you are fallen,
you are wearing the weight of a karmic song.

Be still a moment.
The heat will come to you,
a mother's grief will come to you. Seventy-two bodies become one,
an obliteration.

You have taken to dredging lakes at night - moonlit netting
and dead-heading before the frosts come.
You are on your knees scooping out petals and dead dahlias,
one by one, until light breaks.
Your sleep is stained by the bulk of a Blue Whale.
You even commemorate a garden of city flowers
in their names
yet nothing will suffice unless time itself is reversed.
Look in the mirror and ask who you are again,
and from where the sickness came.

...

.

..   ..

Roiling in the green,
a supermarket trolley
beached in the shallow.

Il Telefono Giallo Nella Casa Gialla
(Dopo Van Gogh)

Un dito leccato attraversa la fiamma.

Facce che diventano di cera immerse
nella luminosità degli schermi e marchiate all'osso,
la mente è un marinaio itterico che naviga
nella foschia, un corpo nuovo.
Una chiazza di petrolio riflette la luna d'oro
avvolta in una corteccia di silicio,
come quei frutti di gelatina
che hanno ucciso i bambini di qualcun altro.

Una frenologia corrotta sciama in alto nell'etere
io grido *smettete di tatuare mappe sui nostri scalpi*
non sapete che lo zolfo diventa color oliva, col tempo
e mangiare uova di passero è un falso antidoto.

Ascoltate.
Ad Arles, Vincent mangiò la digitale
e tutto divenne girasoli
fiore genera fiore e lo stesso il suo orecchio andò perduto.

Yellow Phone In The Yellow House (After Van Gogh)

A licked finger passing through a flame.

We wallow in screen-shine
tallow-faced, & marked to the bone
mind like jaundiced sailors in sun-fog
navigating a new body,
oil slicks reflecting golden moon
held in a transparent cortex of silica, like fruits in jelly
that someone else`s children have died for.

A corrupt phrenology is imposed -
stop tattooing maps on our scalps,
the sulfur will turn olive over time
& eating sparrow yolks as art
is no antidote.

In Arles, Vincent ate digitalis
& everything was sunflowers,
flower begat flower & still his ear was lost.

Blue Period

I find I am getting off at the wrong stops to avoid
the demise of my mother.

I think about the video sent through,
she's cross-legged on the floor behind a play-house,
nails painted cerulean, as modern as the day.

I've always loved his blue period she'd say about Picasso,
Aztec beads bright in her ears, speeding through her town.

She is playing on my nephew's toy keyboard
looks up, laughing at the camera.

None of this makes sense as I imagine her billowing heart
corseted by drugs

and how that must feel inside of you
when you still have ocean nails,

and I wonder what happens
if you're young at heart for all of your life,

what then?

Cameo Brooch Of A Young Woman

Old sun booms through her hair,
canonising her fade.
She is agate-pale,
drinks white tea with no calories,
a reflection in glass.
Soon the hem of morning is unpicked,
she faces unpleasant details,
bleached piss on pavement,
deadlines and meals of falling-apart-flesh.
She stares at the azalea petals,
eyeballs are giant gobstoppers, sucked to a shine,
knocking around in the Pearl White of a spacious mind.
She lifts a glass tumbler of milk and pretends to drink
all the while thinking of whale blubber and Reykjavik in spring
and how those wild flowers decorated
Lady Chatterley's pubic hair.
In the thick of the Zinc White day, she sighs,
waiting impatiently for the ticking approach of night
when she can shine without effort, at ease.

Erosion

THE FAMILY GRAVE OF
ALEXANDER McGONAGALL (ROYAL VICTORIAN ORDER)

THIS HEADSTONE WAS ERECTED
IN THE MEMORY OF
MARGARET GAIL ESMERALDA
THE BELOVED WIFE
OF THE ABOVE MENTIONED
WHO DIED NEAR HERE NOVEMBER 20, 1871
WHEN OF 67 YEARS
(KNOWN TO FLORENCE NIGHTINGALE),
ALSO TO THE MEMORY OF BEATRICE GRACE
DAUGHTER OF THE ABOVE PASSED TOO EARLY ON
DECEMBER 12, 1880,
&
ALEXANDER TIMOTHY MCGONAGALL
WHO DIED ON THE 27TH DAY OF JANUARY 1882
AGED 80 YEARS,
ALL REST IN PEACE

Erosion

```
        HE        G AVE
  G               O         O      D

        HEAD
              HE
        R   A    G   E          D
        HE   LOVED
                      MEN
     H    E   NE           VE    R
            W                 A S
     KNOWN
        S       HE   EM       B        RACE
 D    H


              IM                ALL
     I     N


                      PEACE
```

Table Settings

Is signing a will an invitation to Death
Is Death a sugar skull to be eaten
Is eating fruit enough to stave away cancer
Is cancer a blighted star sign
Are stars still there when you look at them
Is looking an act of archiving
Are archives of value
Is value of value
Is there value in circular logic
Is the exit from circles photography
Is a photograph more accurate
Is accuracy a measure of truth
Is truth measured by beauty
Is beauty for dogs
Are dogs heart-openers
Are hearts dormant until you love animals
Are animals more alive
Is life a measure of connection
Is connection isolating
Is isolation splendid
Is splendour a many coloured plumage
Is a many coloured plumage worn by Death
Is Death more welcoming than family
Are family aware of the future
Is the future full of cosmonauts
Are cosmonauts full of consolation
Are consolations enough
Is it enough that the glass is half empty
Is emptiness desirable
Is desire an invitation
Is an invitation sufficient for Death

Breathe

I can't

It's just a matter of air
coming in
and leaving when you let go
I say

I / can't / let / go

those four words
stained and worked by lips too chilled

fuck the golden thread
I think
what about the eye of this invisible needle

breathe
I say
ride my breath, jump on
I'll take you where your chest will bloom,
remember?

yes
but / this / edge

means we can see where to go
so hold my hand now

Athens Is The New Berlin

There are worse situations to be in
than at a coffee bar, wasting time
in a small airport beyond the fields

falling in love with the notion of home;
imperfections of dead flowers,
cold water in the shower system

and salvaged rubber bands -
lavender and blue, sitting in the kitchen
waiting for their moment of utility.

Away was what we dreamed of
staggering about after dark
screwing the Iliad up against the wall,

we left - halflings seeking Ouzo
to locate ourselves in this dusty Acropolis of salt,
wrapping Midas fleece about our minds,

eating raw honey and blinded by art
but all the while a strange longing
building in the basement of the soul,

written in immured graffiti
in squatted ateliers
and punctured by the burning of passports,

a longing for a drawer of useless rubber bands
and a beautiful broken chair
to sit on at the day's end.

Green As Supreme Emperor

Hair is pulled back into shocked water,
a summer syrup of algal bloom.
Does green transcend beauty?
On studying your eyes I am invalidated,
their shade shifts beyond constraint or reproach, is beatific,
like the way we made mistakes in youth,
tears in locked rooms, walking-outs & walking-ins
cheap bars, absinthe, swallowing, when really
we longed to hold hands, vibrate to a permanent deep green
where we could lucid-dream of
when the planet eats us alive & there's no need for medicine...

The last streaks of day,
lavender hues reflecting
off bright cannisters.

Dinner for One

They had all received the invitation.
Under the harsh strip- light
the selves shuttered away how they felt,
leaving little to peep at.
The food was heavy
in mouths tasting of yesterday,
small mountain scenes built on old plates
as they talked.
How was your day?

The day was long and unaccountable
replied the oldest self. *Like a snake.*

The youngest self flashed back
*The day was furious and bright, we cannot bear
this wasted tenure. Now dance!*

The middle self, calmly -
*The day was tender and momentary, each
flower was watered.*

The great meat at the centre of the table
lifted its heavy eyes and commented
*You are all architects, yet none of you build together.
That is the problem with memory.
You divide and conquer time but
there is enough time for us all. Now dance.*

The knives and forks clapped
and the napkins flew off the table like swans.

Old Ladies of the European Countryside

Curiosity scaffolds their bodies.
They desire digital watches,
trophies on softened folds of skin,
the shock of missing teeth in smiles
like a flash of insight.

A collection of eggs in a perfect basket.
Don't be fooled, each from a different bird,
foul-mouthed and careless
or poetic and still (without make-up)
Stories of falling down the mountain,
poisonous herbs, shot-gun affairs
and the birth of a two headed steer.

Bones as old as silica, light as spring,
tiny movements more precise than a compass.
Pink nylon scarves cradle hair,
their scent is of potato dug straight from earth
radiating from their hot oven clavicles.

Gardens as rich as the sea bed.
Below the dock and nettle lies a fine clay,
unspoken of, a rare knowledge.

Red Eggs

(after Anne Carson)

On Monday I bled so hard & feeling light
saw a saint in the Rorschach blot of Scarlet Lake
my ankles blown by a mischief-maker on crack
messy & careless, I thought
as my eyes grazed a magazine cover of a shining-haired woman
& I craved eggs & protein & spitting at people
in the mirror I checked for wings
in case like Geryon I was mountain-born &
only a hatchling & could return
to that hot space

519 People

519 people died whilst at their work desks this year. The statistics reveal that employees who had been at the same workplace for more than ten years were ten times more likely to expire in this manner, and that more artists died in their 'day jobs' died than any other category of primary occupation. A team of scientists analysed the position of the bodies as found on the desks:

60% were reaching out for something in the moment, 21% writing reports that appeared to be turning into poems and 10% had been trying to leave their desks. 9% had disappeared within the minute after death. In these cases, there was a very faint outline of the body in fine ochre dust, and the scent of violets. The first person to pass away in this manner was writing a treatise on "Making a Fool of Death" complete with woodblock illustrations from an unpublished 18th Century Hungarian occult manual. In this arresting work, small men with elongated noses enter into discourse with winged mice. In a double-page spread entitled Underworld of Labour, there sits below the floor of a wedding banquet hundreds of bent figures toiling over production of armour and weaponry, their gaunt rib-cages and perpetually hungry eyes gleaming in the pale light. At the bottom right of this picture, women try to --pass themselves off as men, betrayed by escaping breasts and grabbed at by other workers.

The last person to die in this manner within the financial year was a fine artist working as a paralegal in The City. The night before she died, she was working in oils on a self-portrait, wearing an exquisite floral coronet of cosmos and floating grass-heads (which remains unfinished).

The advice for concerned readers is to consider hot-desking and drink green tea, high in antioxidants.

A relaxation app linked to this study is also available to purchase.

Making The Most Of Space

Homeless, she rented her body. A prudent act.
Entertaining lodgers was vital, challenged false comfort
& required twin disciplines
of accommodation & decluttering.
Exposed the unoccupied mansions of others
as an abuse of space
detracting from care & awakenings, tugging the soul
away from the body.
The walls of her house were covered in inked flora,
the inner chamber bedecked with rose velvet.
Smoked glass lampshades hung at staggered levels in her head.
She garnered a modest income, knew it was cruel to charge more.
Her Court of Human Rights had judged deprivation of intimacy
as inhumane, like sentencing new-borns.

Alone, she walked her empty rooms to hear
the sighing floorboards, ran fingertips
over flocked wallpaper to feel indecipherable forms.
She would read *Genet* & feel liberated & befriended.
She dreamed of more books, one after another
falling into her home.
She photographed thoughts, filed them away in the loft.
On winter nights she'd write about each, a digestion
as the house aged. She delighted in the art of it all
& when the house was boarded up, derelict,
there was a light flooding the landscape,
a roving beacon for miles & miles,
illuminating the muscle & spume of waves & hills
light from a good soul
    light from a good soul
        light from a good soul

(Dedicated to those buried at Crossbones Graveyard, Southwark)

<u>Note on the poem</u>
Making The Most Of Space is based on a conversation the author had with a sex-working mother about survival and reclamation of self, and the exceptional kindness, compassion and insight she held.

Falling & Seeing Language

The cigarette end glowed,
made tiny golden rain as she threw it to the ground.
She started to run, was late, always late
(in the book she is reading this signals narcissism)

Wind carried a fine mist, drunken birds flew across the street,
seemed like earth was opening up in unexpected ways,
trying to talk, revive an old language.

Abruptly, she fights to catch her breath, she has tripped, is falling

down

the

steps,

moving through the air,
everything slows
down.

She recalls her early time experiments as a child.
Moving steadily to see if seconds could be stretched,

walking and looking into a mirror held
face-up to the ceiling,
floating across inverted terrains punctuated
by zero gravity lampshades, pale puffballs,

to answer the question, *does being inverted alter your sense of time?*

She is grateful that her parents had left her alone.
Interference in development is dangerous under certain conditions,
making fast meals like a pressure cooker.

The catapult shifts her perspective,
she sees herself
moving across the clay blue of the sky like a tiny doll
relative to everything for miles around,
like in an opera or Victorian novel.

She had taught Dickens for many years in schools across the city,
sees that she too is a character,
ebbing and flowing at the whim of the city`s machinations
only dreaming of autonomy.

Heart in throat,
being seen like a splash of blood against the grey sky,
wanting to be unseen, aching at who would be seeing this,
the singular act of falling.

Something pulls at her heart like the witch doctor on the jungle
        suspension bridge
in *Indiana Jones and The Temple of Doom,*
her heart feels like it is coming to the surface,
feels ready to leave, blushing, lavender-hued
it is bleeding sighs, bleeding that she never had a chance to visit
        the Venice Biennale,
to learn to paint, wear dungarees for a year, to sip tea with toasted
        almonds like
in the great French books.

Who would hold this muscle in their clenched fist?

Or, to whom would she make a donation of it?

Conrad for his Heart of Darkness
Or the mute boy on the Reading train when she was fifteen
Or her friend who was made entirely of music and ether
Or her mentor who taught her to see the interdependence of everything
like some sort of Greek oracle?

She could even see inside of the heart, the glimmering muscle,
the power,
the necessary order of transit through the chambers, the flush.
Heart has memory. Transplant recipients have new life and
harbour old life too,
another life within their own. How companionable perhaps.

The heart as motif, I will wear my heart upon my sleeve - the
bard as oracle or life-coach.

The Queen of Hearts, that's what she had been.
Nothing lofty or extraordinary, except that kindness is the best
magic her mother had always said.
The best magic for what?

She feels strings vibrating all over her body - some of silk,
others more like hessian, coarse, pulling her in all directions,
        she is trussed up.
The strings are accountable for the distortion of time and she thinks
she sees an albatross, an echo of the Ancient Mariner.

No filmic series flashing before her, this is a messy collage,
no - not even that - this is a becoming of all things. A resting
    place of being.
A keeping of everything in mind, alive and humming.
Spent her whole life searching for this to find it loitering at the exit...

Flying, soaring high about the Zoroastrian moment,
with joy - feels like bursting, finds she is laughing,
        the colours around her
pulse fresh off the surface of trees, sky, heart.

It is raining luck.

Here is her daughter coming into focus,
their conversation is faster than a heartbeat, elastic, shining,
starts with apology.

At this opening there are hailstones
droplets in her voice condensing in thick sky and bouncing,
hard, to her sister, for being so absent and distracted,
to her partner for being irritable with his habits
even to Dog for not walking her in the rain
and many, many more sorrys in ice, bouncing all over
        the pavement
                off the windscreens of parked cars,

colder than death, the old blue of a glacier is conjured near her face

and she, squinting, tries to see through the tiny lines of fissures
as if they were a reading.
There's not a way of seeing through this,
it`s like being inside a moon opal, a trickery of paths, a poem.

The glacier is making her gasp for breath.

What exactly is it?

Everything blurred and slowed like a concussion.

The pavement is accelerating toward her, this is all she can see
and think of

the fear of pain is redder than the fear of death and smells of salt

swimming in nausea and innervation,
startled circuitry that is shorting.

Heart is jumping like a lab rat,
body tight in anticipation of final contact.

Slams, slams into it, crashes and breaks into it, awakens into it,
smashed to smithereens, human wave breaking on rocks, broken

Head is joining   with   air.

Right hand is far away.

Chest is opening   and closing

like a soft lipped clam at the bottom of the ocean

Some voices, cloud-like, water condensing. *Are you alright? Can you hear me?*

Softness.

Are they looking at her body?   [she cannot see her own body]

cannot tell if her chest is crushed or open,

not an invitation, not a spectacle, she is her body and her

body is in parts and is

moving
through blue light

You Are Wondering About The Past Life Of The Radio Anthropologist

as you are driving
through a place
and are suddenly hit
with this intense and sad fondness
for the names of Cul de Sacs
and the persistence of an old hotel
the idea of the Marina
lights up your calves and biceps
full of bright nylon cupping the wind
you realise that
you long for this place
every single day
because you lived here
when everything was alright
things that are further away
should be blue
this is learned at Art School and
shading one side of a person's profile
will lift it into solidity
which is what you are doing
to this memory
you notice
there have been
a multiplicity of points
to diverge from
like the ultrastructure of a feather
you have no idea
if any of those tiny paths
would have preserved
the time when everything was alright

no matter how many times
per second the wing beat
the whole notion of
when everything was alright
is ridiculous
like a banana you have no appetite for
and is a terrible symbol
it is also like those magic eye pictures
where you can't see unless
you force yourself to relax
and abruptly
you are let into another world which
disappears again
but now you know of it
and find yourself staring at nothing
for hours on end

in hope
which takes the form of a pink tulip
in a perfect red vase the shape of an egg
you are feeling tired
and think about sitting at a bar
bathing in neon shining through
constellations of bottles on shelves
you are remembering
how swimming blurs memory
holds it at bay afloat
if the sea were nearby
you'd rather bathe in the cold
day or night in a heartbeat
but the sea is for rich people
and whelks only opening

on occasional Sundays for you
like the Dim Sum Palace
under the bridge
in your garden
there are many bees
and they have deserved you ten-fold
they make porcelain of the sky and
drip honey into the cosmos
through glass tubes
the hospitals are sighing from them or
maybe it is the other way around
it is a new time
the time of bees
and you are trying to
forget when everything was alright

Gaia in the Live Lounge
(COVID 19 Pandemic 2020)

I am driving to see my mother
playing lottery with a small chance
of killing her there are so many ways of
killing by love and this is just one version
I think of monogamists in perfect kitchens
letting the water run out of modern taps
and soft kittens crushed by children
and people who feed ducks with supermarket bread
when the sun shines and female bodies
limp on the floor and I think that maybe
the worst of all these sad things
is killing your mother because
there is no greater location of love

that is love's first home
unspoken or full-sung mother is the sky
above your head and cracking panes
of thin glass and cold water and fever
a flock of swifts flew over my car turning
a page and the real sky was
cornflower-blue tinged with dazzling violet
and the air was clean with spring
and I felt the terrifying sign of earth's power
and how she had tolerated my near killing of her
until she'd had enough and turned
knowing that it is worse to raise murderers

All like decaying fruit,
collapsing softly inward.
Dreaming of the sun.

ACKNOWLEDGEMENTS

• 'The Thoughts Of Valerie Solanas' was published as an earlier version by *RxPoetics Magazine* (Rough Night Press) 2018, rebel editor Win Harms

• 'Athens Is The New Berlin' was first published by *MIROnline* June 2019

• Section 2 in an earlier version was first published in *RxPoetics Magazine* (Rough Night Press) August 2019, edited by Win Harms

• 'My Identical Twin' was first published in the anthology *Alter Egos* (Bad Betty Press) editors Amy Acre and Jake Wildhall, August 2019

• 'Vocal Tics' and 'Table Settings' were first published in *Datableed* September 2019

• '519 People' was first published in the *Mechanics` Institute Review: The Climate Issue. No. 16*, September 2019 and later in Aesthetica Creative Writing Annual December 2019

• 'Pink PV15 part 1' was first published in the anthology *Fool Saint* edited by Michael Curran (Tangerine Press) March 2020

• 'Elite Members Of The Momentariat' was first published in the anthology *Smear* edited by Greta Bellamacina (Andrews McMeel, US) in April 2020

• 'The Party' was shortlisted for *The London Magazine* Short Story Prize 2020

• 'Yellow Phone In The Yellow House' was translated into Italian by the incredible poet, editor and translator Cristina Patregnani and first published in *Rivista Literary Magazine*, September 2020

• 'Making The Most Of Space' was published as an earlier version in the anthology *When They Start To Love You Like A Machine You Should Run* - New River Press Yearbook 2019, editor Heathcote Ruthven

• 'Gaia In The Live Lounge' was first published in the anthology *The Language Of Salt* (Fragmented Voices)

- 'Hair' was accepted for publication in *Poetry Review* due Winter 2020
- 'The Pill' was accepted for publication in *Vessel* due out January 2021
- 'Baba Yaga In Her Life As A Teacher' was accepted for publication by *SAND Journal*, Issue 22

Thanks, in no particular order, to Denise Saul, Ana Seferovic, Sam Hacking, Amy Acre, Kirsty Allison, Win Harms, Cristina Patregnani, Tamar Yoseloff & Shazea Quraishi for encouraging and supporting my work in unique and meaningful ways. Also to the Poetry School for my education in the micro-specificities of language, and to my friends for their support, especially Polly and Kate.

A thousand thanks to Stuart Bartholomew of the incredible Verve who persuaded me that I could do this and believed in my work.

Personal thanks to my beautiful family. This book is not possible without you, Sol and Marlon

ABOUT VERVE POETRY PRESS

Verve Poetry Press is a quite new and already award-winning press that focused initially on meeting a local need in Birmingham - a need for the vibrant poetry scene here in Brum to find a way to present itself to the poetry world via publication. Co-founded by Stuart Bartholomew and Amerah Saleh, it now publishes poets from all corners of the UK - poets that speak to the city's varied and energetic qualities and will contribute to its many poetic stories.

Added to this is a colourful pamphlet series, many featuring poets who have performed at our sister festival - and a poetry show series which captures the magic of longer poetry performance pieces by festival alumni such as Polarbear, Matt Abbott and Geraldine Carver.

In 2019 the press was voted Most Innovative Publisher at the Saboteur Awards, and won the Publisher's Award for Poetry Pamphlets at the Michael Marks Awards.

Like the festival, we strive to think about poetry in inclusive ways and embrace the multiplicity of approaches towards this glorious art.

www.vervepoetrypress.com
@VervePoetryPres
mail@vervepoetrypress.com